Moments from the Side Yard

I ... you love p... I hope you enjoy these Moments Angela Bell Julien

Painted Poetry & Prompted Journal

Angela Bell Julien

Moments from the Side Yard: Painted Poetry & Prompted Journal

Published by Wheatmark®
2030 East Speedway Boulevard, Suite 106
Tucson, Arizona 85719 USA
www.wheatmark.com

ISBN: 978-1-62787-840-1 (paperback)
ISBN: 978-1-62787-841-8 (hardcover)
LCCN: 2020917239

Also by Angela Bell Julien:
Blooms and the Bard: Painted Sonnets
Trees Don't Rush
(Mind Your Moments Series: Book One)

To my daughters:
Wendelyn Rene Julien and Francie Jane Julien-Chinn.

They epitomize visionary, hard-working, gentle souls—the theme of this book of poetry and journal prompts. Their strong spirits hold me upright. Both of them inspire, encourage, and support me in all I do.

Special acknowledgements go to:

Marcus Reinkensmeyer for photographing all of my paintings,

Daniel J. Julien, Ph.D. for editing my writing
and for his insightful feedback.

Paul D. Julien for his editing, feedback, encouragement,
inspiration, love, and patience.

Contents

Part Three: "Gentle Souls"

Foreword

I am not much of a planner. In fact, I struggle to see life as a straight line where one moment leads directly to another. My lack of planning has sometimes led me to take circuitous paths to find the way—only to find that "the way" didn't really exist, but the alternate route was exactly where I wanted to be! As a child I was called a "daydreamer." As a teen I was "inattentive." As a professional, people often kindly refer to me as a "random thinker." I prefer to think of myself as a "creative spirit." No matter, I love it when things serendipitously come together.

As I assembled the pieces of this new book, I struggled with a title and creating order among the "moments" I had collected. Serendipity struck! I am an avid fan of stories with characters who are unusually brilliant and put seemingly unrelated clues together to solve problems. I also tend to late-night binge watch television series that match those plot lines. While watching a third or fourth episode of one of my favorites, the main character, a quirky genius, found the need to explain to a friend the definition of "moment." I had forgotten that "moment" was a physics term!

In physics, a **moment** is the effect of a force that causes an object to turn around a chosen pivot point.

Metaphorically, this definition of "**moment**" perfectly describes the ideas expressed in *Moments from the Side Yard!* Life is all about the effects of forces that help us see the world from multiple points of view— moments that bring us joy and others that make us reconsider our current situations. Taking time to absorb the energy of the moment is what lifts us, holds us up when the spinning gets too fast. Staying anchored to a pivot point keeps us from flying off course, reminds us to stay true to ourselves. In *Moments from the Side Yard,* Mind Your Moments: Volume 2, the poems, paintings and journal prompts will take you on a journey that helps you find your own energy and gives you the opportunity to feel the thrill of centripetal force!

My side yard is my "pivot point." I learned to love a best friend there; I learned to hit a baseball there; I found peace and solace there and sang songs to myself—loudly. I wrote poems there; I found my voice there. My side yard and the forces that helped me pivot around the world from there have led me exactly here—somewhere I never expected to be. I hope you enjoy *Moments from the Side Yard* and that in it you recognize the energy that moves you to destinations you have not yet planned.

The Beginning...

Moments from the Side Yard is written in three parts, each follows from the title poem.

I realize that combining physics terms and poetry is a little odd. However, I hope you will enjoy the juxtaposition—I am as surprised as you might be about the synchronicity of the two.

Each painting is followed by a poem and each poem by a journal prompt with lined pages for you to write your own thoughts. I hope you find many special moments!

The Side Yard

A time to reflect,
Standing alone
    The sun has made the
Stone in the yard—a grill
    Cooking the bottoms
Of my feet.

They will be oven-red soon,
But I struggle to make them move.

The tree is trying desperately
    To shade me
And I wonder what I have done
To deserve the cooling kindness,
    —a funny tree
With a straight trunk, and
    Dr. Seussly bent branches
Holding toothbrush leaves.
I want to see it laugh—
    I am sure it does
When I turn away.

A partial pivot on the stone
    And I am Alice

Looking in the glass—
But mine is brilliant silver in
    The sun.
Rays make it shimmer opaque.
No one can see the one inside
    Sitting at the kitchen table
With an old-fashioned newspaper,
    Working the crossword puzzle.
No one knows she worries what will come
With tomorrow's wind.

I do not worry. I turn again and
    look intently
At the blossoms—blooming plants contained in
    pots and beds—still
Growing wildly,
Peering out at myriad heights
With flower faces attempting to be
    First to see the sun.

The cacti are volunteers—seeds brought
    On a bird's wings,
The fluff of a rabbit or the foot of a bee.

I stand in what they call "the side yard."
My favorite
The side yard, where
I can choose to let my feet

Cook and enjoy
The simplicity of life.

I am neither front nor backyard, not so
    Well-defined as that.
Like the tree, I stand straight,
    But wiggle
In the wind.
I love to stretch and feel
    The sun,
Not considering symmetry or style
Yet finding safety in the
    Proximity of home.

I am happy here. Tomorrow's winds
Will come, worry
Or no.
In the clouds' gentle voices,
I can hear my grandmother
    Wistfully sing
"Que sera, sera"
And my mother whisper
In my ear,
    "with visions inspired,
 hard work,
And a gentle soul…
The future is yours
—you see."

Where is your pivot point? What keeps you centered and inspired? What are the most important forces on your moments?

_____

_____

_____

_____

_____

_____

_____

_____

_____

_____

_____

_____

Part One

…And my mother whisper
In my ear,
   "with

Visions Inspired,

 hard work,
And a gentle soul…
The future is yours
—you see."

Visions Inspired

"Visions" is perhaps just an adult word for daydreams. My mother indulged my daydreams, my visions, my "creative spirit." She chased the end of the rainbow with me, made costumes for characters I chose to be, inspired me. She grew up in Oklahoma during the Dust Bowl. Life was tough, but she and her family worked the land to sustain their lives while many others moved away. Her keen attention to what farming did for her family allowed her to have creative visions to help others. She left the farm after high school and forged ahead using her uncanny math skills as a book-keeper, and she modeled for a major department store.

Years later, she and my father traveled around the world and enjoyed becoming part of many new communities. When living in one particular community, she found a group of people in desperate need. Hunger was weakening their bodies and their spirits. She reached back to those early learnings—long lost daydreams of the beauty of a garden growing. A vision was inspired!

Using her considerable persuasive skills, she acquired 500 baby chicks, sent from thousands of miles away, and a plethora of seeds and seedlings to start a farm. Her warm heart won over some of the skeptics in the group and soon she became a mentor, a collaborator, and an extra pair of hands. Her creative thoughts gave the community the strength to develop their own vision. They built a farm, developed skills and became self-sustaining. Often, visions inspired, daydreams, are dismissed as whimsical. The whimsy of life can be the impetus of great accomplishment!

Inspired visions are the force that initiates "moments." They are not "6th senses" or some special gift. They are the result of paying close attention to what you see, think, and feel and then dreaming about what it all means.

Wishing you many visions inspired!

Into the Hand I Hold

Her strength
Runs through me.
Straightens my stance,
Squares my shoulders.
Often, I can feel her,
Seeing with my eyes,
Clearing my vision
—rather than the path.
In the mirror, I watch
Her unwavering
    countenance
But when I turn away,
I know the weakness
That must have been
    hers, too.

How could I have known
The hand with which
She so sturdily
Pulled me through life
Was her balance?
—that my resistance
Held her upright and
Built the muscle
Of her powerful influence
Over those she touched
Her strength
Runs through me
Into the hand I hold.

What is the muscle of powerful influence you have over others? What would you like to send through your hand into the hands you hold? What has been sent to you?

_____

_____

_____

_____

_____

_____

_____

_____

_____

_____

_____

_____

Tribute to the Sun

In spring
The desert
     Flames yellow.
Prickly-spined desert flora
Let go the tiny
     Reservoirs
Of water
They have held
     protected
Through the winter
To blanket the
     Desert floor
In tribute to the sun.
Desert interlopers
Muse in what seems
     Magical flair
Until the desert floor
Hits
Solar flames
And the real masterpiece
—an authentic miracle
     Of heavenly art
Brushes across the sky.

I live in a "desert" which evokes an image of an arid scene bereft of beauty; I think that is what makes any burst of color spectacular. The sun's energy moves me to see how truly dynamic nature is and makes me think about how changing my "colors" might evoke the same magic in me—and sometimes move me out of a "desert" state of mind. What helps your dreams "hit the solar flames" and become dynamic? How does it give you energy to move forward?

_____

_____

_____

_____

_____

_____

_____

_____

Come Swing With Me

Please take my hand and swing
With me
Let's giggle to the sky
Above the tree
We'll work our ropes
—Defying gravity,
The breeze will set us free.

Please take my hand and swing
With me again
Retake our youth
—Remember "then."
Push off with dreams
envision a new "when."
Futures to begin.

Please take my hand and swing
with me,
We'll push and pull and find a
Perfect harmony,
Taking risks and reaching high
Tethered safely as we fly.

Laughter therapy has proven to be an effective medicine against heart disease and other afflictions. I believe it also inspires great visions…those who laugh heartily certainly inspire me! Who would be your "giggle to the sky" partner, someone who makes you giggle when you think of them? Why? Close your eyes and imagine swinging together as children—what are the dreams you could renew?

_____

_____

_____

_____

_____

_____

_____

_____

Purple Nights

Tickled light
> Mirrored night

Mind seduced
> Ascent induced

Crest sought
> Balanced thoughts

Equipoised incline
> A vertical spine

Purple mist
> Nipping kiss

Enchanted sky
> Echoed reply

Tickled light
> Mirrored night

"Enchant" is one of my favorite verbs! I have realized that being "enchanted" is a choice I make—and when I make it, creative thought absolutely flows through me, but I have to give away some sense of realism to do so. As a child I was often enchanted by the night sky, of weaving in and out of the stars. What enchants you? Why?

_____

_____

_____

_____

_____

_____

_____

_____

Flower Music

Flower music
    Transcends
The lines
    Drawn upon
      Pages,

Meant to
    Order
Notes and
    Control
      Chords.

Flower music
    Trills
Asynchronous
    Tunes,
      Whistling

Melodies of
    Joy
Textured in
    Bashful
      Rhythms.

Flower music
    Enrapts
The soul
    Softly.

Painting the
    Timber
Of the
    Garden's
      Dew.

Sometimes inspired visions fit neatly inside the lines. Sometimes they do not. We are often taught that coloring inside the lines and making music in perfect keys creates beauty. I have come to find that I cannot create within the lines—that experimentation leads me to a more divergent use of the lines—and that sometimes I fit new definitions into old lines—and sometimes I don't. More importantly, I have realized that art is best when it fulfills a dream of the artist, not because it is acclaimed by others. Where are you most comfortable, inside or outside of the lines? What fulfills your dreams?

_____

_____

_____

_____

_____

_____

_____

_____

_____

Superstitious Skies

Superstitions
> Whisper through

Scorched air
> Visible in waves

Of heat, live in
> Alcoves shaded

And moist
> From last season's

Rain—held in
> Secret

To support
> Awkward, unexpected

Life.

Biotic homes where
> Seeds hide

And take root
> Bearing life

So strong
> It weakens

Stone
> And spreads

To the mountain's
> Edge

Where it finds the solid
> Sky, metallic,

Burnt and copper
> Shimmering with

Superstitious truth.

Superstitions do odd gymnastics in my mind. Are they extensions of our visions, requiring us to take precaution or give us extra strength? What allows you to take on new feats, move to the mountain's edge?

_____

_____

_____

_____

_____

_____

_____

_____

_____

Serenity and the Plot

Serenity breeds
    Awe and wonder.
Shade is near,
    Light afar.
Gentle lapping against a
Bright yellow kayak
Hums a story
    Written in a million
Uncapped waves
    A plot that either
Breaks ashore to find
    What lies within the
trees
Or moves
    With the water
Toward more distant
    Destinations.

Serenity breeds
Imagination as
The kayak glides
    In silent dialogue
Slipping into mystery

Where storm and
Tempest lay in wait.

Serenity breeds
    Temporary restoration
Before the tale's momentum
    Rises into
White and whirling water
    Inciting passionate
Exploits or perilous
    Quests,

Before the craft slides
    Evenly into a
Denouement of insight.

Serenity breeds
 the moments
That launch the saga
    And moor the epilogue
Safely home.

Although change is sometimes quite frightening, I find that the only reason for serenity is to prepare us for it. Without change, we would have no story. I must admit that given the choice, I probably like to stay close to my pivot point. I am so grateful for the forces in my life that have moved me into tempests and white water causing new dreams and visions, but I am always pleased when I find the new, revised calm as well! What forces in your life move you to venture into the trees or to take the water to destinations you cannot see? What are some "moments" that have made your story worth telling?

_____

_____

_____

_____

_____

_____

_____

_____

_____

_____

Gems

No busy travelers
Pass by,
…The dirt road
Has no sign,
Just a hand-hewn fence
Built with sweat
…and six packs.

From a distance
Drivers see dust,
…and more dust…
And a simple abode
With wooden poles
Holding up a
Tin roof.

Nothing encourages them
To make the turn
…venture up the hill.
They are chasing
"the sights"
Or wealth
…or status.
They miss
The treasure—the jewels
A closer look discloses,
…the view of amethyst

Mountains sliding
Into the horizon
Is set below
Citrine clouds
That glitter
Across the sky
—just there for the
Taking…in.

In the evening
The dirt road
…turns golden
As emerald
Prickly pear
Guard the little
House.

A turquoise portal
Opens into a
Room of
Rose quartz.
…Glowing love.
The search ends here
For me
…surrounded by
Gems.

During my life, there have been times when I would have turned down the dirt road, and times I was just too busy. Seeking gives our brains purpose. Seeking and curiosity is how we build visons. What are you seeking right now? Will you turn down the dirt road or move on to find other paths? Where are your gems?

_____

_____

_____

_____

_____

_____

_____

_____

_____

_____

Orange Explodes

The sun sets in
Earth's obligatory
Turn

Every day of
Every year, it
Burns

A promise of
Tonight's stars
Unbroken

Enlightened touch
Between day and dark
Unspoken.

Silently dressing
The horizon's edges
Found

Enchanting hues never
Cease to startle
—Astound
In waves of iridescence.
Brilliant orange
Explodes

Disseminating dusk
Upon the globe
Bestowed

Glory in the
normal journey
spinning

Secrets stored,
Quietly awaiting a
New beginning

Remember, in physics, a "moment" is the effect of a force that causes an object to turn around a chosen pivot point. Every day is an earth "moment" as the planet rotate around its axis. We can trust it; we can know the sun will come up and set, yet every day we are awed by glorious sunsets. Not all visions are unexpected, some are ordinary, although so majestic that we do not grow complacent. What brings you awe in your normal life? What do you see, hear or feel every day, and never tire of? How does it inspire you?

_____

_____

_____

_____

_____

_____

_____

_____

_____

Dancing Leaves

Sometimes there just is no
Deep meaning

Sometimes the moment
is just about
The flowers
and dancing leaves

Sometimes our minds
Should leave the depths
To find
Simplicity.

Rest in the softness
Of the petals
Relish in the comfort
Of the scent
Content with nothing
More.

Some moments are difficult to define. I can't always talk about what I am thinking because I am simply taking in the moment. Time in my side yard does this for me. What are the simple pleasures that just let your mind relax? How often do you let yourself fall into them?

_____

_____

_____

_____

_____

_____

_____

_____

_____

_____

Electric Time

I remember
>> Yesterday's blue
And yearn for the
>> Yellow of tomorrow,
>> But
Today makes me wonder…
>> What is now?
The present cannot exist
>> In a breath
It is past
>> And less than a
breath ago it lay in the
>> Future
I keep grasping,
>> Trying to hold on
To the moment.

A silver wisp of
>> Time
Feels electric in
>> My hands.
I cannot keep my grip,
>> Yet I relish
In the current,

Like the foam
>> On the ocean,
There…a sparkle
>> ….Gone
A forward moving
>> Ripple.
I endeavor to adorn myself
>> In the froth,
Lather in it
>> ….Search its
countenance.
I do not breathe
>> —still,
The mystery remains
>> Time
Eludes and disappears.

Time mystifies me. This is one of my favorite daydreams. How do I catch the moment? People talk about "living in the present." How do I do that? Is this the moment? Can I travel in time? Is that what memory is? What do you think about time? How do you "hold the moment?"

_____

_____

_____

_____

_____

_____

_____

_____

_____

Part Two

…And my mother whisper
In my ear,
   "with visions inspired,

hard work,

And a gentle soul…
The future is yours
—you see."

Hard work

If my mother was the protector of my creative spirit, my father was the model of work ethic—and combining that work ethic with creative thought. They were quite a pair! He was a civil engineer, often hired to build roads or bridges or pipelines where others couldn't. He built a road in Panama through rugged terrain intended to connect Central and South America. He put a pipeline in the Sahara Desert. He loved to talk about his work. At dinner, we sat and listened as he drew diagrams on napkins and solved geographical and mathematical problems to build his current project.

I did not choose to follow his path, but I did choose to be my own thinker, to not let others influence me, to work hard and make my own pathways. Napkins became my manuscripts; the first draft of much of what I write.

My father dreamed big—and sometimes he made those dreams happen. He made me believe I could make dreams come true—if I worked hard. Or, I could dream big, work hard and fail (the rainforest reclaimed part of the road he built in Central America—nature was a force greater than he) relearning and attempting again, and again. Always being right didn't matter; the dream and the work mattered.

Hard work invigorates me.

The Back Side of the Sunset

I come to this
Place
Often
To talk with the
Saguaro.
He is old and
Wise;
He knows to
Bask
In the
Moonlight
Without asking
Questions.
I stand near him,
Watch
As he reaches to
Touch
The color of the
Back
Side
Of the
Sunset
The mountains'
Shadow
Reaches out but
Leaves
Enough
Light

For me to feel
Rich
In golden
Rays.
I tell him of my
Weary
Day's
Work
He stands
Strong
Encouraging
Me to
Meditate,
To mind the
Moment
To follow his
Lead
Until unconsciously I
Dance
In twilight's
Melody,
My spirit and the
Moon's
Embrace.
I am home.

Everyone loves the front side of the sunset. The back side doesn't get much attention—even though the colors in the east can be just as vibrant. After a day of hard work, I find that great moments happen when I am not looking in the expected place. That weary-bone feeling puts me in just the right place for looking away from the bright light gazing into the rising moonlight and chatting with a friend who only listens. Where is your favorite unorthodox place to find a special moment? Who do you talk to "in the moonlight."

_____

_____

_____

_____

_____

_____

_____

_____

A Force Multiplied

Work simplified
Is energy transferred
—A force multiplied
By the distance desired.

But work purified
Is the spark and plug
—The fire applied
To life's endeavors

Hard work extends
the muscle and the soul
Vitality ascends
within exhausted minds

Moment and motion
Synchronous power
Of mortal devotion
Purpose personified.

According to Merriam-Webster—and a patient college physics professor— "Work is equal to the amount of force multiplied by the distance over which it is applied. The unit for measuring work is the same as that for energy in any system of units, since work is simply a transfer of energy."

I love that feeling I get when I have truly transferred all my energy into a purpose—when I have "gone the distance" to achieve my goal. How do you transfer energy to achieve your purpose? Where do you find your "synchronous power?"

_____

_____

_____

_____

_____

_____

_____

_____

_____

_____

Time to Climb

Breathe

Inhale...lung-filling

          Penetrating

Brain aerating deep

          Breath

Oxygenated pulses

          Behind panoramic

Eyes of

          Yellow optimism

Tracking ascents

          Ahead

Exhale...toxins

          Disbelief, fear, worry

Cleansing viral

          Doubts

From mind

          And muscle

Purged, purified

          Confident

Absolute, resolute,

          Forward

Brace

Stretch…extend

        Horizons

Along silver lines

        Of risk

Contemplate

        The journey,

Pathways, stumbles

        Triumphs

Sense transformations

        Extend views

Enfold…equip

        Means,

Nourishment, patience.

        In white clouds

Of hope. Gather

        Fortitude

Humor, Grace

        From quondam

Travelers

        Unite

Break out

Wander…among

        The trees

Find dignity, awe

        Humility

Ponder divergent

        Paths.

The map directs

        And binds.

Witness more

        Enjoy ambiguity

Grapple…With the

        Precipice

Reach, resist

        Temptation

To hide amid

        Security

Complacency—creating

        Vapors

Scramble over rocky outcrops

        Ignite

Bear On

Fight…not the

                Clock,

Own the hours of deepest

                Labors

Travail the steep

                Arduous and tough.

Spirit rises when

                the body's

Muster weakens.

                Revive

Sing…to the trail's

                Rugged melody

Gain cadence

                Of heart

And mind

One-step, one-step,

                One-step

Waltz

                In thin air.

The moments when I press so hard that my body complains are some of my favorites. When I work or think so vigorously ideas blur or muscles ache are moments when I am on creative overload. I daydream as I hike, I doodle as I think. What do you do when you overload your senses? I waltz; how do you dance?

_____

_____

_____

_____

_____

_____

_____

_____

_____

_____

The Dove

The white dove labored long
To build her nest.
Her tireless employment
 inspired me.

I watched her use nature's scrap
Pulling, tugging, working, weaving
Until the tiny abode fit perfectly
Atop the wooden ledge
just outside my window

She made my daily duties lovely
-delicate-
I smiled knowing she was out there
toiling with me.

Evening came, and I retreated to my
Own nest.
—less precariously perched, but
Similarly
affected by outside winds.

Within my own, I controlled the wind
And slept—dreaming of the bird,
Craving her strength; her freedom;

Her beauty.
Day *re*woke and shuffled me back
Through
The wind—to work.

As I walked, I saw much debris
Of man
had escaped the broom
And blower
Over night.
Plastic bottles, cigarette butts
—saved for posterity;
I grimaced,

Back to my routine
—But today,
Today
I had a friend
…The dove.

My peaceful ally.

So, I went to the window
Pulled gently on the string
And slowly lifted the brittle
blinds.

Oh!

Such dismay!

The nest had not escaped
The broom.
All signs of the dove and
Her undertaking
Were gone
As though her struggle
Had been only in my mind.

The glass had
Allowed us to share
Unafraid.
But the world
Could not bear it
…She and I
Together we might
Have been too strong.

I am left to wonder
If her work
Could be so easily
Discarded

…What of mine?

Doves symbolize optimism. What we know about the dove is that she went to a different sill and began a new nest never pausing to think that her work was in vain. I am inclined to overthink my situation, to question the direction of my moment. Moments of reconsidering force me to adjust my efforts and check to ensure that my work fulfills my creative spirit and aligns with my pivot point. Do you have an optimistic ally? What experiences have made you reconsider your path? How do you align to your pivot point?

_____

_____

_____

_____

_____

_____

_____

_____

_____

Part Three

…And my mother whisper
In my ear,

　"with visions inspired,

　hard work,

And a

gentle soul…

The future is yours
—you see."

Gentle Souls

A gentle soul puts others before self, spends the moments of life seeking ways to make the world a better place, not necessarily in monumental movements, but in daily practices that form bonds and provide nutrients for moments otherwise unborn.

Gentle souls leave a permanent impression. I have been blessed by many gentle souls passing through my life and leaving me better for spending precious moments with them. They have taught me patience, insight, and have attempted to teach me grace. They are often those we forget to thank; those we realize much too late have formed our lives; those who ask for nothing in return. Here, in this unforeseen path of mine, I want to extend that gratitude to all those gentle souls who have cared for me, who have given me their hand when I most needed it.

As you read the following poems, think of the gentle souls who have touched your life and how you have touched the lives of others.

Colossal Kindness

Fragile blossoms
Bloom atop strong
Arms protected by
Thick and thorny
Spines.

Light catches
The petals as they
Perch precariously
Floating above aged
Limbs,

A delicately
Woven nest cradles
In the notch
Carved in the giant's
Skin.

Feathers faintly shaded
Camouflaged
For safety,
The Jenny protects her
Chicks

A hummingbird
Flutters, circling
the spongy arms
Seeking sweet nectar's
Syrup.

Fearing nothing, tiny wings
Helicopter there
Until they and
The breeze, waft
Away.

The desert
Behemoth looms
—A royal surveying
The noble
Realm.

Not to gender power,
Rather, to offer
Its colossus
To shelter the
Meek

And tender charity.

Who are the gentle giants in your life? Not giants necessarily in size, or in power, or influence, but perhaps in character—or propensity for love. What gentle giant would you like to talk to? What would you say?

_____

_____

_____

_____

_____

_____

_____

_____

_____

Aloft

Once tempered strong to hold more weight
than light,
A solid orb with crystals metered tight
Lacked beauty, shape, interpretation of
Purpose, worth, and duty's occupation

An emptiness within a solid sphere
Just taking space upon the shelf of fear.
Until the gaffer's twists unveiled a vase
So elegant with waves of silken lace,

A fragile charm of gilded, soft-blown glass.
Emboldened by molten color's heat,
An open marbled globe; an artist's feat
Splendor valued for such elegance —alas

Age is measured not in glory, injury or cost
But in the strength to hold the frail aloft.

As our experiences mold us and make us look for beauty or for wealth, with time we find true value. Interesting, how moments take on their own energy when they are fueled by empathy, by compassion, by grace. To hold others aloft is a gift we give ourselves. Describe a moment you held someone aloft and a moment someone held you aloft. What did you learn from each?

_____

_____

_____

_____

_____

_____

_____

_____

_____

_____

Plain and Simple

It's about time

        To see the planet's

Pain

It's about time

        To accept the truth

—Plain and simple.

Earth

        And all its wonders are

—Overused

Beyond that,

        With wanton carelessness

—Abused

It's about time

        to see our planet's

Pain

It's about time

        to accept the truth

—Plain and simple.

The oceans

        Have borne debris of

Humankind

The atmosphere cradles

        Toxic fumes for our

Peace of mind

It's about time

        to see the planet's

Pain

It's about time

        To accept the truth

—Plain and simple,

        unredacted

The fragile orb must be

        Protected

There will be no

        future harvests if

uncorrected

It's about time to see

        The planet's pain

It's about time

        To accept the truth

—Plain and simple.

Collective

        Minds can curb the

Loss

The earth can't wait

        There's been too great

A cost

It's about time

        To see the planet's

Pain

It's about time

        To accept the truth

Plain and simple.

The globe

        Needs a soft

Embrace.

Before we lose our footing

        In all of time and

Place.

Forces that cause an object to turn around a pivot point may send that object in the wrong direction if the forces ignore the wind that brings them. We live on a fragile orb that has provided us with the nutrients of life for all of humankind. Where is your favorite place on earth? How has it nourished you? What steps do you take to nourish it?

_____

_____

_____

_____

_____

_____

_____

_____

_____

Looking into the Light

Optimism
> Is not blindness
To the world's turmoil
> And pain.
Like a prism
> It bends the light
To unveil the rainbow
> Curved in the sky
Opposite the sun,
> Drawing arcs
Of hope and gratitude.
> The mind's own
Refraction
> Determines
Dazzling and darkness
> Challenge and defeat
Looking into the light
> Changes the view.
Allows eyes to see
> The spectrum
Free from notions
> Preconceived, unbiased,
Prepared to accept
> Brilliant opportunities
>> of light.

I believe optimism is the keeper of the energy that moves us forward together. Optimism allows us to see the light and look for brilliance. How do you stay optimistic?
What do you see when you "look into the light"?

_____

_____

_____

_____

_____

_____

_____

_____

_____

Night Lights

The river roils,

White caps, lit

        by what is left of day.

The mountain just a silhouette

without dimension

        as dusk encroaches.

The sky turns deep

Reaching back to

        Primordial time

While the flowers

Vernal, free

        and bright

Provide the night

With a glimmer

        Of light.

During times when my energy has been spent, and I cannot feel the moment, times when my pivot point is hazy, gentle souls provide me with just a little light—just enough to lift my spirits. Imagine the glimmer of light in your life. Where is it? How do you revive after a "roiling river" day?

_____

_____

_____

_____

_____

_____

_____

_____

_____

Tangerine Spirits

Deep life
Sways in the current
Causing watery illusions
Of scarlet blooms
And days are lovely.
Life moves with the current

Until, a tangerine spirit
Interrupts that life,
Streaks through it
Invigorating emotions,
Opening eyes
Electrifying static

And the course of
Days is never the same.
The spirit moves on
But the water has changed;
The flash of energy
Has permeated hearts
Making illusions real

Tangerine spirits come into our lives, make us better people, and then move on. They are those bright flashes that leave indelible marks behind our eyes. Take a few moments to list the tangerine spirits from your life. Write each one a quick note, just one sentence each. Tell them about the mark they left behind your eye.

_____

_____

_____

_____

_____

_____

_____

_____

_____

_____

The Only Tree

The sand burns

    My feet

But I cannot

    Find the will

        To move

I am entranced

    By the

Magnitude of

    Deep green

        Mountain ridges

The song

    Of the singing sea

Has lulled me

    Transfixed

To ignore

    An impending

        Storm

Still standing

    On the prickling heat

Of shards of shells and glass

    I watch the

Island, as though

    It might suddenly

    Disappear.

As though the storm-cloud's

    Shadow

Has made it

    Mystical

        Ethereal

    Temporal.

I cannot take my eyes off the tree

    …the only tree

Emerging from the island's core.

An oxymoron of

    Fragility and

        Fortitude,

Enlightened by

    The magnitude

Surrounding it.

A palm that bears
    Sturdy fruit
In the side-yard of the scene
    Steals away
        The thunder
Of the storm
    And reminds me
To stand
    Firm
Even in my own
    Seemingly simple
Side yard.

If the energy sends us around a pivot point,
we must eventually return to our beginning.
Our personal revolutions find us fragile, find us fierce. I just want
to go back to my side yard and stand under the tree. Are you
fragile? Are you fierce? Are you ready to return to your side yard?

_____

_____

_____

_____

_____

_____

_____

_____

_____